Zac and Chirpy

Story by Annette Smith
Photography by Lindsay Edwards

Rigby®

A Harcourt Achieve Imprint

www.Rigby.com
1-800-531-5015

Here is Chirpy.

Here comes Zac.

3

"Come here, Chirpy,"

said Zac.

"Come to me."

"No, Chirpy! **No**!"

said Zac.

"Come here!"

8

"Chirpy! Chirpy!" said Zac.

"Come here.

Come to me, Chirpy."

Look at Chirpy.

Look at Zac.

"Here, Chirpy!" said Zac.

"Come on.

Come here."

Here comes Chirpy.

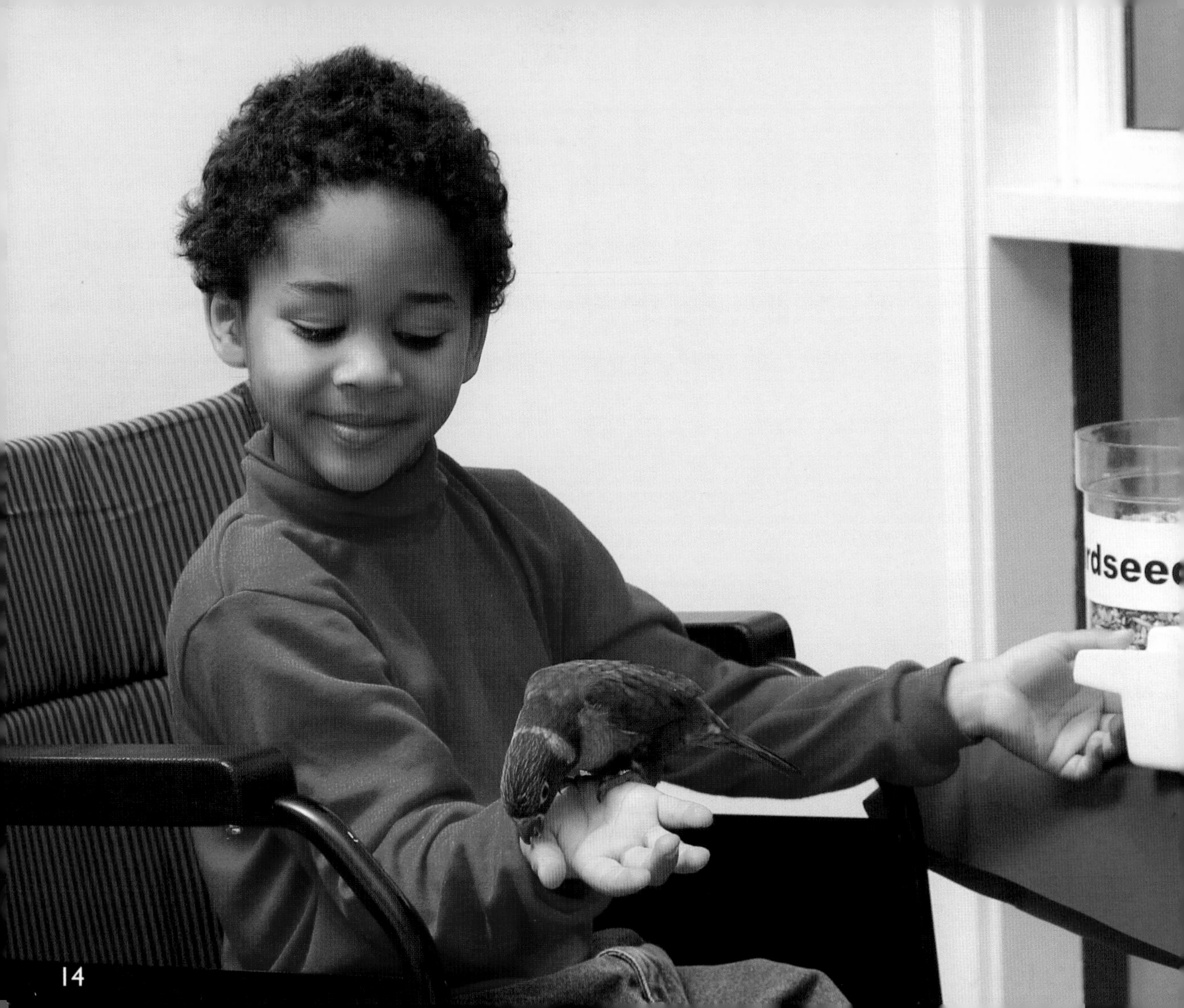

"Chirpy is on my hand,"

said Zac.

"Dad," said Zac.

"Look at Chirpy."